Overcoming the Emotional Trauma of Divorce with God as Your Guide

Gwendolyn Carlton-Haynes

Disclaimer

The content of this book—including text, graphics, images, and other material—is for informational purposes only. Nothing contained in this book is or should be considered or used as a substitute for professional medical or mental health advice, diagnosis, or treatment. Never disregard medical advice from your doctor or other qualified health care provider or delay seeking it because of advice you have read in this book. I urge you to seek the advice of your physician or other qualified health professional with any questions you may have regarding a medical or mental health condition. In case of emergency, please call your doctor or 911 immediately. The information contained in or provided through this book is provided on an as-is basis without any warranty, express or implied. Any information utilized from this book is voluntary and at your own risk.

Warranties and Limitation of Liability

This book is presented for use by the general public without warranty or guarantee. The author is not liable to any user or anyone else for any decision made or action taken based on reliance upon the information contained in or provided through the book.

The author does not make any express or implied warranties, representations, or endorsements of any kind (including, without limitation, warranties of title or infringement of third parties' rights or any warranties of merchantability or fitness for a particular purpose) with regard to the services, or with respect to any information, product, service, merchandise, or other material provided in or through the service. The author does not warrant or guarantee the accuracy, completeness, correctness, timeliness, or usefulness of any information, services, or other material provided within this book.

This book or parts thereof may not be reproduced in any form, stored in a retrieval system, or transmitted in any form by any means without the prior written permission of the author, except as provided by copyright law of the United States of America.

Unless otherwise noted, scripture is taken from the New King James Version®. Copyright © 1982 by Thomas Nelson, Inc. Used by permission. All rights reserved.

Author Image: Glamour Shots

Contact the author, Gwendolyn Carlton-Haynes, at haynesgd@hotmail.com.

CONTENTS

ACKNOWLEDGMENTS

This book is dedicated to my family and friends. I love you all. Without your love, wisdom, patience, encouragement, and support, this book would not have been possible.

I will lift up my eyes to the hills
—from whence comes my help?
My help comes from the Lord,
who made heaven and earth.

(Psa. 121:1–2)

INTRODUCTION

I don't remember what was said leading up to the words "I want a divorce" escaping from my husband's mouth; however, I can recall my physical reaction, it felt as if the breath had been knocked out of me. For the first time in my life, I didn't know how to respond because I never expected to hear those words from him. I believe that even in the worst marriages, it's always a shock when one partner actually takes the first step toward ending the relationship. Instantly, questions began to formulate in my mind: When did our marriage become so intolerable that divorce was the only solution? How long has he felt this way? What happened to us?

I still smile when I think about how happy we were at the beginning of our marriage. We actually enjoyed being together. How could he forget about those times when I would wake him by sitting on the edge of the bed, leaning over him, and then gently tickling his lips by brushing against them softly with mine? I would sit totally amused, watching his lips involuntarily twitch in response. Becoming aware of my presence, he would slowly open one eye and then the next, only to find my smiling face peering down on him. Pretending to be annoyed with me for waking him, he would say playfully, "Leave me alone" while trying desperately to keep a smile from emerging at the corners of his mouth. He would then lovingly pull me toward him, encircling me in his arms, holding me snugly against his chest. I felt so loved.

What about those times in the middle of the night when we would move toward each other in bed, sleepily smile at one another, embrace, then kiss, drifting back into sleep, bodies entwined hand in hand, face-to-face? I felt so desired. How could he want a divorce when every day we would say, "I love you" and kiss good-bye as we departed for work? And what about those times when he would wait patiently beside the garage door just to give me a kiss as I entered the house? It seemed like we were always joking and laughing. I felt so appreciated.

Finally regaining my composure, I asked him if he was sure he wanted a divorce. To my despair, his answer was yes. Thus began my journey through divorce.

I soon learned that going through a divorce—whether you are at the beginning, in the middle, or at the end—can be at times both mentally and physically taxing. That is why I decided to write this book. I wanted to share with you, how the Love of God helped me let go of the negative emotional trappings of the past, and move forward with my life. It is my hope that by the time you finish reading this book you will have learned

- how the presence of God in your life is the key to over-coming adversity
- how to respect the free-will decisions of others, and

- that you have the power to release yourself from harboring negative feelings by embracing this time of change in your life as an opportunity for growth

This book is arranged as follows:

Chapter 1 Seeking God's Face Addresses the importance of establishing a relationship with God and offers techniques on how to incorporate biblical principles into your day-to-day activities.

Chapter 2 Free Will Defines free will, discusses how each individual has a right to make his or her own choices in life, and addresses how the way in which we evoke our free-will decisions (walking in the Spirit vs. walking in the flesh) can have a positive or negative impact on the lives of others.

Chapter 3 Obtaining Professional Counseling Talks about the importance of seeking professional counsel to assist you in overcoming the trauma of divorce and provides a checklist for determining which professional counselor best suits your needs.

Chapter 4 Negative Emotions Identifies negative emotions commonly experienced before, during, and after a divorce (disappointment, shame, guilt, resentment, hate, and anger) and offers coping techniques to aid you in minimizing and/or eliminating those emotions' impact on your life.

Chapter 5 You Gottas Encourages you to let go of your hurt by forgetting the past, forgiving those who hurt you, and focusing on moving forward with your life.

Each chapter includes key lesson indicators. These indicators summarize the material presented in each chapter

- **What the Bible Says** - Biblical principles that correlates to the topic discussed are provided at the beginning of each chapter
- **Take-Away** - A summary of important lessons appears at the end of each chapter.
- **Emotional Benefit** - Suggested emotionally satisfying actions appear at the end of each chapter.

CHAPTER 1:
SEEKING GOD'S FACE

Chapter 1: Seeking God's Face

What the Bible Says:

I love those who love me,
and those who seek me diligently will find me.
Riches and honor are with me,
enduring riches and righteousness.
My fruit is better than gold, yes, than fine gold,
And, my revenue than choice silver.
I traverse the way of righteousness,
In the midst of the paths of justice,
That I may cause those who love me to inherit wealth,
That I may fill their treasuries. (Pro. 8:17–21)

How many times have you talked with someone who has gone through a divorce and because of the pain expressed so vividly on their face, you assumed that the divorce must have been recently, only to discover as the conversation concluded that the divorce took place years ago?

During one such conversation with a friend, I remember thinking, "*Why can't she just get over it?*" I have to admit, I never understood how emotionally painful divorce could be until I experienced it myself. I soon learned that "*getting over it*" isn't a simple task.

Divorce is emotionally traumatic because it's an immediate lifestyle upheaval. In a short period of time you are forced to deal with

- the breakdown of your marriage
- obtaining legal counsel
- negotiating major life issues such as:
    - child custody
    - parental rights
    - spousal and child support
    - maintaining Life and health insurance coverage
    - shelter
    - equitable distribution of the marital assets
    - who is responsible for the marital debt

while at the same time attempting to sustain a normal life.

What you quickly discover - is that you are ill-prepared, to handle the physical and emotional toll of working through a divorce. In fact, some people are so scarred by the experience -they continue to relive the feelings of hurt, and pain which they encountered during such a volatile period in their life - years after the divorce has been finalized.

I didn't wish to become that angry person vividly reliving the hurt and pain of my divorce. So, I made a decision at the beginning of the divorce process, to establish objectives to keep me focused on ending the relationship amicably, expediently and walking away from the marriage not harboring any remorse, hate, or anger. I decided to

- weigh the consequences of my decisions prior to taking action to ensure that my behavior (words and deeds) was reflective of the presence of God in my life
- focus on those things I could control—and forgo those things out of my control
- conduct myself with dignity and treat others with respect so that when the marriage ended, I could walk away from the experience happy, healthy, and looking forward to starting a new life.

It felt great to focus on the positive, letting go of the negative. However, there are times in our life that even with good intentions it's impossible to do the right thing without help from above. I'm talking about divine intervention. For me to achieve the objectives I'd established for myself, I had to connect with the greatest source of strength and inspiration—God. I needed to connect with God because only God could change my heart.

How Do You Connect with God?

One night as I lay awake in bed, I began to pray. I asked the Lord to lead me in the right direction because I felt so confused and lacked vision. His response: *Seek my face and not my hand*. Here's my interpretation of what God was saying to me

- you are not alone. Know that you can come to me for healing and advice by opening yourself up to me. Invite me into your life, and I will send my
- comforter, the Holy Spirit to stand by your side, and guide
- you through the challenges of life
- you can reach out to me any time not just in times of adversity. You can connect with me through studying my Word (the Bible) so that you will
  - understand who I am, and learn about the sacrifices my son Jesus made in order for you to have a better life
  - obtain knowledge, vision, and power
  - discover who you are, and use my teachings as a guide for fostering
  - better relationships

Clearly, God wanted my attention. It's funny, as a child I found it easy to connect with God. Connecting with God seemed natural. I think that our young hearts and eager minds, still pure, are more open to experiencing new things without judgment or fear. I felt that God always answered my prayers and I could always feel his presence around me, but as I became an adult, just like everyone else, the only time I sought guidance from the Lord was when I was troubled. I had to ask myself, how would I feel if the only time I heard from members of my family or friends was when they needed help? The answer: unappreciated. God was telling me that he desired my uninterrupted attention. He wanted to connect with me not just in time of adversity but in every way, every day. God wanted me to come back home. I got the message. The reality was I was lost, lonely, and had been feeling empty inside for some time. I welcomed the opportunity to reconnect with God.

So, how do you seek God's face? Simple, when God sends you an invitation...**RSVP!**

R = Repent - confess your sins to God. Ask for forgiveness and accept the fact that God has already forgiven you.

S = Seek him diligently — invite Him to come into your life and guide you. The Bible says to put God first in your life.

V = Vow - make a decision that you believe in God, and will follow Him with all your heart, and soul.

P = Pray — reach out to him through prayer. Praise Him by singing songs of praise and worship

Now that you have accepted God's invitation to allow him to come into your life, take action to make the relationship stronger. Here are some options to get you started:

• **Study the Word.** The Bible is the key to understanding and connecting with God.

The more you learn about the Word, the closer you will become to God. As your connection with God grows, your desire to read the Bible for inspiration and guidance will increase. Use the Bible as a reference (template) for how to live your life. Don't be afraid of the Bible; use it just like a textbook. Jot down questions or scribble your thoughts in the Bible. It's OK to circle, underline, or even highlight scriptures in the book. If you are really serious about earning the Word, purchase a Bible dictionary or concordance to assist you in interpreting scriptures or researching specific topics.

Emotional Benefit: Change requires action. It's true that the more you learn, the more you'll grow. You can't benefit from the wisdom in the Bible, unless you make the decision to implement, what you learn in your day-to-day activities. Taking action gives you a sense of empowerment. When you focus on positive things, you attract positive energy into your life.

• **Humility and prayer**. Another way to spend time with God is through humility and prayer. Humble yourself by letting God know that you are nothing without him in your life, and you need him for guidance, love, affection, and protection.

Humble yourself so that you can hear God's voice, be open to receiving his word as fact, and not challenge his guidance. Humble yourself by letting go of your free will, and succumbing to God's will.

Emotional Benefit: Praying allows God's love to enter your heart and soul. When you humble yourself, you will be capable of receiving wisdom, opening up your heart to give, and receive love.

• **Got church?** What does going to church have to do with connecting with God? Church is God's house. Church is where

- you learn how to pray and how prayer connects you to God
- you learn how to read and interpret the Bible and you learn the importance of incorporating biblical principles into your daily life
- you learn about mercy, compassion, and the power of forgiveness
- saints come together to inspire one another

Emotional benefit: Attending church will teach you how to build and maintain a relationship with God. Additionally, most churches have a myriad of counseling services, support groups, programs for divorced, single adults, single parents as well as youth groups which will give you, and your children the opportunity to connect with others who might be experiencing the same life challenges.

• **Multi-Media Ministries.** If you can't, don't have the time or don't like attending church then an alternative is to fellowship via televised, on-line webcasts or radio ministries. Advantage

- flexibility – most multi-media ministries are available 24 hours a day 7 days a week (check your local listings)
- available on all mediums
  - websites
  - webcasts
  - pod casts
  - audio and video tapes
  - radio stations
  - electronic mail (email)

Emotional Benefit: Connecting with God is a personal journey. You don't have to visit a brick and mortar building to connect with God. God is everywhere. Do what makes you feel comfortable. The goal is to get connected to God because He is your healing source. God will heal your broken heart, give you peace of mind, help restore your faith in yourself, and in others.

• **Serve others.** Whenever, I begin to feel sorry for myself, I look for ways to help others. When you do unto others you are doing unto God. Serve others and become a source of light in the world by

- reaching out to family and friends and asking if you can be of service

- volunteering – offer your time and talent to non-profit agencies in your area
- hosting a Bible study group in your home, or getting involved in a community project. Find a need in your neighborhood and then create ways to fulfill that need

Remember, your plans don't have to be *grand*; they just have to be *enacted*.

Emotional Benefit: You become a higher level of yourself when you reach out to others.

Spread love into the world and you'll receive love in return. You'll learn that the world doesn't revolve around you. I know it's shocking but true. Besides, it's therapeutic to get over yourself and into helping others. It's good for the mind, body, and soul.

• **Continuous learning.** There are a variety of forums available to assist in creating and sustaining a relationship with God

- participating in Bible study groups
- attending religious conferences or retreats
- establishing an independent study program for yourself by
- purchasing inspirational books, audiotapes, ebooks, CDs, and DVDs
- or study aids (such a Bible concordance, or Bible dictionary)

Emotional benefit: Learning new things keep you alive. It inspires you to take chances, to see life from a different point of view. Watching, listening to, or reading inspirational material (it doesn't have to be religious based) then applying what you have learned to your day-to-day life will give you the strength to let go of negative thoughts, replacing them with a positive outlook on life.

What's the Payoff for Including God in Your Life?

Well, in addition to what Proverbs 8:17-21 offers the most important payoff for making God a part of your life is Agape love. What is *Agape* love? I define it as unconditional love (pure), the love that God (the creator) has for you (the creation). What are the advantages of having an Agape (relationship) with God?

A = Affection (bond) between you and God that can't be broken

G = Guidance from the Holy Spirit

A = Acceptance (unconditionally) by God

P = Peace, hope joy, happiness, and prosperity

E = Everlasting love

Take-Away: By now you are probably asking yourself, what does establishing a relationship with God have to do with overcoming the emotional trauma of divorce? It's simple

If	Then
You want to rebuild your house	You must connect with God to ensure that the foundation is strong
You wish to be healed	You must connect to God, your healing source
You seek wisdom	You must connect with God by studying the word (Bible), and incorporating what you have learned into your daily activities
You wish to build a relationship with God	You must **RSVP** to God's invitation

Emotional Benefit: Only God can change your heart. When you invite God into your life you open the door to happiness, peace, love, joy, and freedom from carrying past burdens into your future.

So far, you have been encouraged to build a relationship with God. The next step in setting the foundation to *Overcoming the Emotional Trauma of Divorce* is to realize that sometimes we can't control the actions and/or decisions of others, but we do have the power to control ourselves. What I'm referring to is **free will.**

CHAPTER 2:
FREE WILL

Chapter 2: Free Will

What the Bible Says:

For I know that in me (that is, in my flesh) nothing good dwells; for to will is present with me, but how to perform what is good I do not find.

For the good that I will to do, I do not do; but the evil I will not to do, that I practice.

Now if I do what I will not to do, it is no longer I who do it, but sin that dwells in me.

I find then a law, that evil is present with me, the one who wills to do good.

For I delight in the law of God according to the inward man.

But I see another law in my members, warring against the law of my mind, and bring me into captivity to the law of sin which is in my members.

O wretched man that I am! Who will deliver me from this body of death?

I thank God—through Jesus Christ our Lord! So then, with the mind I myself serve the law of God, but with the flesh the law of sin. (Rom. 7:18-25)

Wow! Talk about being conflicted. When I first read these scriptures, I could feel the inner turmoil erupting from Apostle Paul's words as he tries desperately to suppress the endless conflict in his head between wishing to do what is right and succumbing to selfish desires. You can only imagine how frustrated Paul must have been when he finally proclaimed, "*O wretched man that I am! Who will deliver me from this body of death?*"(Rom.

7:24) Does this tug of war between right and wrong sound familiar? It should—these scriptures are a perfect example of free will.

So, what is free will? My definition: Free will is the power and freedom to decide your own path. Because God has given us free will, we have the innate ability to decide what is right or wrong for ourselves in any given situation without his interference. God does not make us follow him; it's our choice. However, the irony of making free will decisions is that we- and inadvertently others-have to bear the consequences of the decisions that we make.

Why is it Important to Understand Free Will?

Because whether you are working through a divorce or facing the emotional aftermath there will be questions that will remain unanswered. Therefore, the sooner we learn to accept the fact that

- we can't control or predict the actions of others
- there will be times when our lives will be affected negatively or positively by free will decisions made by other
- we may never receive an answer to why someone has made a decision that we didn't wish for, don't understand, control, or appreciate

The happier we will be in life. Once you embrace the concept of free will, you will discover that you have the power to

- accept, respect, and survive the free-will decision of others
- make good choices when evoking your free will by incorporating Godly principles into your decisions

Evoking Free Will

The method in which you evoke your free will is broken down into two categories: Walking in the Flesh, (Works of the Flesh) and Walking in the Spirit, (Fruit of the Spirit).

What the Bible Says:

I *say then: Walk in the Spirit, and you shall not fulfill the lust of the flesh. For the flesh lusts against the Spirit, and the Spirit against the flesh; and these are contrary to one another, so that you do not do the things that you wish. (Gal. 5:16-17)*

Behavioral Characteristics associated with Walking in the Spirit vs. Walking in the Flesh are as follows
- Walking in the Flesh, (Works of the Flesh)(Gal. 5:19-21)
  - adultery
  - fornication
  - uncleanness
  - lewdness
  - idolatry
  - sorcery
  - hatred

- contentions
- jealousies
- outbursts of wrath
- selfish ambitions
- dissensions
- heresies
- envy
- murders
- drunkenness
- revelries, and the like

- Walking in the Spirit, (Fruit of the Spirit) (Gal. 5:22-23)
  - Love, joy, peace
  - long-suffering, kindness, goodness
  - faithfulness, gentleness, self-control

Examples 1 and 2 below demonstrates the how the way in which you choose to evoke your free will decisions can impact the lives of others.

EXAMPLE 1

What happened?	You receive an unexpected request from your in-laws to Visit the children.
Holy Spirit guidance:	Do the right thing and allow the children to see their grand-parents.
Your decision:	I know it's wrong but I don't want to see them because I'm still angry about the divorce.
Categorize Your behavior:	Example of Walking in the flesh (hatred).
Correlating Biblical Principle:	*For the good that I will to do, I do not do but the evil I will not do, that I practice (Rom. 7:19).*
Impact of Your decision:	Because, I didn't allow my in-laws to visit the children the relationship between the families are now strained.

EXAMPLE 2

What happened?

I deliberately picked a fight with my ex-spouse for no apparent reason. I know my behavior is wrong and I don't wish to behave this way but I'm so angry!

Holy Spirit guidance:

Seek professional counseling to deal with my anger issues. call my ex-spouse, and apologize for my behavior.

Your decision:

I've decided to obey the guidance of the Holy Spirit. Even if the apology is not accepted, the reward is in being obedient. I am grateful that the presence of God in my life keeps me focused on doing what is right. I began researching counselors in my area so that I can learn coping tools to help me control my anger.

Categorize Your behavior:

Even though the initial action was an example of Walking in the Flesh (Outbursts of wrath) by being obedient to the Holy Spirit it changed the outcome to Walking in the Spirit (Goodness).

Correlating Biblical Principle: *I find then a law, that evil is present with me, the one who will to do good. (Rom. 7:21)*

Impact of Your decision: It hurt my pride to apologize but in the end, I felt relieved. My spirit was lightened from removing the guilt of my bad behavior, and I was able to let go of the anger. My ex-spouse accepted my apology, and we now have a better relationship.

It is important to understand free will and the difference between walking in the Spirit versus walking in the flesh because throughout the divorce process there will be

- many circumstances where your **moral** fortitude will be challenged and you'll have to decide if your reaction should be based on fleshly needs or spiritual influence
- instances when you should **contemplate** prior to taking action how your free will decision can impact your life and the lives of others.

Take Away: The only way to overcome the emotional trauma of the past is to let go of the pain.

- Stop
    - spending time pondering "why" and "what if's."
    - blaming yourself for the decisions/actions of others.
    - trying to control others' behavior.

- Start
    - taking accountability for your own behavior.
    - weighing the consequences of your decisions and how they will impact the lives of others.
    - living a higher-level of yourself by creating a relationship with God, following the guidance of the Holy Spirit, and incorporating biblical principles in your daily life

Emotional Benefit: Understanding free will, and how the way in which you choose to evoke your free will decisions impacts the lives of others, gives you the tools necessary to think before you act, and strive to do the right thing, regardless of the circumstances. Additionally, it gives you the grace to respect the free-will decisions of others, even if you don't agree with them.

Now that we have established a relationship with God and defined free will and how it can negatively or positively impact your life and the lives of others, let's take another step toward mental empowerment by **obtaining professional counseling.**

CHAPTER 3:

OBTAINING PROFESSIONAL COUNSELING

Chapter 3: Obtaining Professional Counseling

What the Bible Says:

Listen to counsel and receive instruction,
That you may be wise in your latter days. (Pro. 19:20)

What Just Happened?

As I stated earlier, I was surprised when I learned that my husband wanted a divorce. It felt as if the wind had been knocked out of me. Once, I was finally able to regain my composure, I asked him if he was sure that a divorce is what he wanted, to my despair his answer was yes. At that moment, it became clear to me that what had just transpired was bigger than me. I needed help. To understand how our marriage had gotten to the point of no return, I decided to visit a marriage counselor. To assist me in deciding which marriage counselor would be the right fit for me, I developed a **Counselor/Therapist Checklist** to streamline the selection process. Feel free to use my checklist to assist you in researching professionals in your area.

Counselor/Therapist Checklist

Academic/ Professional Credentials

What professional or accredited training and licensing does he or she have in their area of expertise How long has he or she been in practice?

Services Provided & Affordability

What type of services are available: Psychotherapy, marriage, individual, group, youth or family counseling? Are fees comparable to other similarly qualified Professionals? What are costs per session? Are fees Negotiable based upon patient income? Are payment plans available? What forms of payment is accepted (debit or credit card, cash, personal checks?) What type of insurance is accepted? Will you be charged for late or missed appointments?

Flexibility

What are the business hours? Are late evening and week-end sessions available?

Comfort Level

How did you feel about the counselor after the initial telephone interview? Did the counselor seem actively engaged in the conversation? Did she or he answer your questions to your satisfaction? Did you feel comfortable talking to the counselor?

Final Selection Who are you selecting and why?

For information on the types of professional counseling available in your state check out the American Psychological Association website: http://www.apa.org

Why Counseling?

There are times in everyone's life when the problems we face exceed the advisory expertise of our support system: family, friends, coworkers, or spiritual leaders; it's during these times that we should seek the professional services of a counselor or therapist. A Counselor can help you

- work through your hate, anger, frustration, trust issues, depression, thoughts of suicide
- learn how to love again and release emotional baggage of the past
- get in touch with 'who' you are and 'what' you wish for your life
- develop coping techniques for handling stress

Fair Warning!

Working with a Counselor will not be easy. And, obtaining the desired results will not be expedient. You have to put in the time and effort in order to reap the benefits. Keep in mind that seeking counsel isn't about exposing the behavior of others; the goal of counseling is to obtain a better understanding of yourself and learn how to take ownership for your role in getting to where you are in life. I've found, "*that the hardest glance in my life has been the reflective look at me in the mirror.*" If you need help and don't know where to begin start by reaching out to others for inspiration, guidance, love, and support. But, if you find that you still can't let go of the rage in your heart then seek professional counseling. Don't let foolish pride keep you from getting the help. Seeking the guidance of a professional counselor can be just the catalyst needed to push you toward making a change for the better in your life. After all, the first step toward overcoming anything is about taking action. If you aren't happy with how things are going in your life what are you going to do about it? Change requires: **A Map**

A = Acknowledge - that something is wrong in your life

M = Make a move - take the necessary steps to obtain help in identifying what is Wrong and possible solutions

A = Apply - the coping techniques that you've learned by studying the Word and through professional counseling to solve the problem

P = Position - yourself for success by establishing goals / objectives that keep you focused on creating a new life and meeting new friends

In regards to my situation, although, I did not attend many sessions with the marriage counselor, I found both the individual and couple sessions enlightening. Through counseling, I discovered that it was illogical to think I could be the type of woman my husband needed, and that it was not possible for him to be the type of man I desired. Therefore, divorce was the logical conclusion for our situation. No regrets. No remorse.

Take-Away: The goal of obtaining professional counseling is to help you learn how to **let go.**

L = Learn – that you can't depend on others to make you happy – that is your job.

E = Evaluate – your past and present relationships so you will not repeat the same mistakes in the future.

T = Tear down- those negative mind-sets keeping you trapped in the past, unable to move forward.

G = Grow stronger - by taking control of your life, being accountable for your decisions, as well as your behavior

O = Overcome — feelings of disappointment, shame, guilt, hate, and anger by controlling your thoughts, actions, words, and deeds.

Emotional Benefit: Peace. For some, connecting with a spiritual source (God) can provide all the comfort and insight needed to successfully move forward after a divorce. Others reach out to family, friends, or their spiritual leader (clergy) for the strength, and courage to rebuild their lives after a traumatic event. Yet there are times when only a professional counselor can help identify past and current behavioral patterns blocking your emotional growth and help you learn how to overcome their negative affect on your life.

So far we have established a relationship with God, defined free will, and created a checklist for obtaining professional counseling. The next course of action toward overcoming the emotional trauma of divorce is confronting our **negative emotions.**

CHAPTER 4:
NEGATIVE EMOTIONS

Chapter 4: Negative Emotions

What the Bible Says:

But Jesus, knowing their thoughts, said, "Why do you think evil in your hearts?" (Mat. 9:4)

During the days, weeks, and months leading up to, and after my divorce; I experienced a myriad of emotions triggered by anything, everything, and even nothing. Let's face it; you become one big ball of emotions. Listed below are the negative emotions (feelings) I experienced frequently while going through my divorce

- Disappointment
- Shame
- Guilt
- Resentment
- Hate & anger

In this chapter we will analyze the negative emotions identified above and explore coping techniques, (based upon biblical principles), I developed to help control their impact on my life. First up, **disappointment.**

DISAPPOINTMENT

Disappointment

What the Bible Says:

A merry heart does good, like medicine,
but a broken spirit dries the bones. (Pro. 17:22)

What Happened to Till Death Do Us Part?

"You have every right to be angry!" Those were the words my best friend uttered indignantly to me one night over the telephone. Her usually soft-spoken voice was riddled with anger. I could only listen and cry softly into the telephone receiver, wiping my face with a damp towel as the warm tears continued to flow down the side of my face while she expressed her anger. Listening to her speak so compassionately, I felt loved. When you feel beaten down, helpless, and disappointed, it's good to have someone in your corner that will come out fighting, if need be, on your behalf. She went on to say, "He promised to love, honor, and respect you till death do you part. He did not honor his promise, and you should let him know that you are disappointed."

It's OK to Feel Disappointed.

What she said was profound at the time because until those words were spoken, it never occurred to me that I had a right to be disappointed, or even angry! All I felt was guilt. As I said good-bye to her and placed the telephone back onto its receiver, the reality of my situation hit me hard. I suddenly realized that I was facing a complete lifestyle upheaval. I was being forced to walk away from everything familiar (our marriage, home, family, and friendships), step out on my own, and somehow rebuild my life as a single woman. Well, not single, now a new category: divorced.

Let's face it life doesn't always work out the way we envisioned because we don't have the power to predict the future or control the actions of others. What disappointed me most during and even after my divorce was the loss:

- loss of the marriage, (I had to revise my vision of the future), and
- loss of relationships (I suddenly was abandoned by those with whom felt I had forged lasting friendships)

However, I have discovered that if I believed in free will, then I must respect their decision to depart from my life.

What Causes Us to Feel Disappointed?

I have found that when I've experienced disappointment it was because I was harboring unrealistic expectations about myself, the people in my life, or what constituted happiness.

It took some time, but eventually I discovered that if I wished to overcome disappointment, the first thing I had to do was learn how to accept change. Part of accepting change is to learn how to say good-bye.

Question: How do you **say good-bye to your marriage?**

Saying Good-Bye to Your Marriage

What the Bible Says:

Brethren, I do not count myself to have apprehended; but one thing I do, forgetting those things which are behind and reaching forward to those things which are ahead. (Phi. 3:13)

I never imagined he would leave. Wasn't I supportive of him? Didn't I listen to his problems? Offer him guidance, love, comfort, and support? Didn't I help him realize his dreams? Didn't I create a beautiful home and make sure that everything his heart desired was readily available? I was a good wife! Yet here I am the good wife—all alone!

Those were the words I said to my brother during one of our many tear-filled telephone conversations during my divorce. I lamented how I had given my all to ensure the marriage would be successful, only to have it fail in the end. He listened patiently as I went on and on, feeling sorry for myself, then he said lovingly, soothingly, and very candidly, *"Stop crying. This will not be your last love."* He was right, though at the time it sure didn't feel that way. I simply had to accept the fact that the marriage was over and I alone had no control over its success or failure. You have heard it said before, and it is true—it takes two to tango.

What the Bible Says:

Can two walk together unless they are agreed? (Amo. 3:3).

If only one party is committed to the marriage's success, then it will fail. And there is nothing that you shoulda, woulda, or coulda done that might have changed the outcome once your significant other has decided to walk away. In order to say good-bye to my marriage and remain sane leading up to and after the divorce, I had to embrace some simple truths

- it's OK to *grieve* the loss of your marriage. The end of a marriage can be a dramatic, life-changing experience.
- you can't make someone *love* you. Give it up; it's impossible and demoralizing.
- you can't *hold* onto someone who wants to leave. Trying to do so will only leave you feeling frustrated and hopeless.
- you can't *deny* what your heart knows to be true. Lying to yourself will not change the outcome.
- you shouldn't *compromise* your self-respect. No one will respect you if you don't respect yourself.

My brother was right—no one person can be everything you need. People will enter and leave your life (sometimes by choice, sometimes by force), so to base your self-worth, sense of security, hopes for the future, and ability to be happy on the success of a relationship is unrealistic. Don't sell yourself short; you deserve better. Besides, someone departing from your life isn't always a bad thing. Because people are unique, the relationships you form together are unique. There are times when the interchange can produce dynamic, satisfying, and long-lasting relationships. However, there are situations where the interchange results in a toxic environment, the relationship is held together not by love but because no one has the courage to break the link. Often, in our desire to remain in the familiar, we fail to take a realistic look at life absent the rose-colored glasses.

Take-Away: Don't romanticize the marriage. When it comes to relationships

- respect what you had together, cherish the good times, and learn from the bad
- take what you have learned and use that knowledge to forge better, stronger, healthier relationships in the future; and
- appreciate the fact that as time goes by and you have a chance to heal, you might find that letting go of that relationship or that person was the best thing that ever happened.

Emotional Benefit: The failure of a marriage is a traumatic experience. By taking the time to grieve the loss, you are giving yourself the opportunity to heal. If you don't deal with the pain, you transfer the hurt and anger from the failed marriage into other relationships.

Up next: **Where are all my friends**? How do you handle the loss of friends when the marriage ends?

Loss of Relationships: Where Are All My Friends?

What the Bible Says:

All my close friends abhor me,
and those whom I love are turned against me. (Job 19:19)
As in water face reflects face, so a man's heart reveals the man.
(Pro. 27:19)

I didn't anticipate loss of friendships. Suddenly, people I had known for years, and with whom I had spent what I thought was quality time no longer returned my telephone calls and those who did remain began to act uncomfortable around me. There seemed to be an unspoken separation of friendships and loyalties. Never do the words "his, mine, and ours" seem more apt than during the breakdown of a marriage. When the marriage ends, friendships suffer. Here's what you will likely experience and **What the Bible says** about their behavior

Actions	What the Bible Says
Some friends will readily choose sides, pledging loyalty to one person or the other	*A man who has friends must himself be friendly, but there is a friend who sticks closer than a brother (Pro. 18:24)*
Some friends remain loyal and will be there to comfort you in your time of adversity	*A friend loveth at all times, and a brother is born for adversity (Pro. 17:17)*
Some friends will take advantage of the situation, choosing to pit one side against the other	*Put away from you a deceitful mouth, and perverse lips far from you (Pro. 4:24)*
Some friends may decide to walk away from you both, choosing not to take a risk that your divorce will corrupt their marriage	*My friends scorn me; my eyes pour out tears to God (Job 16:20)*

Don't think that this fight-or-flight behavior is limited to friends. Some family members, especially those whose relationships are in crisis, may choose to limit their association with you during this time of turmoil. Although, this negative reaction from others to end your friendship may be confusing and disappointing, don't take it to heart. This is a difficult time for everyone. Your friends and family are also struggling with how to handle themselves around you and your estranged or ex-spouse.

How Do You Handle Loss of Friends?

If someone chooses to exit your life, you have no choice but to accept their decision. Remember, you can't hold onto someone who wants to leave. Perhaps the individual's departure will be for a short time or forever; either way it's not your decision. Take comfort in the fact that God loves you and he is the greatest friend you could have in your life!

Be grateful.

Learn how to appreciate the people who remain in your life. Sometimes we experience disappointment or may feel abandoned because we simply spend too much time yearning for lost relationships or waste too much time contemplating why people have left. What about the people who have remained dedicated, and committed to your shared relationship? Rather than focusing on the negative, why not redirect your thoughts, and focus on the positive? Why not spend time

- loving those who love you?
- cherishing those who cherish you?
- being loyal to those who are loyal to you?

- forgiving others their transgressions so that God will forgive yours?
- appreciating those who appreciate you?
- accepting the fact that God knows when others' time with you must come to an end? Give thanks to God for looking out for your best interest

Take-Away: Learn from your relationships (good, bad, and ugly). Know that as far as relationships are concerned

- God loves you and that is the greatest love (Agape) that you can experience;
- life changes and people will leave us—say good-bye; and
- when someone exits from your life, use the loss as a window of opportunity for creating new friendships.

Emotional Benefit: Independence. It's important to learn how to stand on your own. True confidence is the ability to allow others the opportunity to be themselves even though the thought of losing them may hurt you in the beginning.

Question: What did you do? Why are you feeling **ashamed**?

SHAME

Shame

What the Bible Says:

And the Lord set a mark on Cain, lest anyone finding him should kill him. (Gen. 4:15)

Marked for Life: The Scarlet Letter D

Raise your hand if you thought at the beginning of your marriage you would be getting a divorce.

Raise your hand if you felt like a failure leading up to and even after the divorce.

Raise your hand if you feel as if a huge **D** has been branded on your forehead.

Raise your hand if you feel a little embarrassed when you have to check the "divorced" box on a document asking your marital status.

Raise your hand if every time someone asks about your marital status you feel a little guilty and find yourself wanting to explain what happened so it's clearly understood that it isn't your fault the marriage failed.

Raise your hand if you feel there is a stigma associated with divorced people.

Raise your hand if after you told your family or friends about your pending divorce you felt like a failure or less of a man or woman for not being able to keep your marriage together.

Now relax, put your hand down, walk over to a mirror, look yourself in the eyes, (wipe the crust out of the corners), then say to yourself, I am not

- damaged property
- a loser
- a failure
- marked for life, or
- a bad person

A friend of mine said to me that after her divorce she felt ashamed. Her self-image was low. She felt there was a negative stigma attached to the word "divorcee." Every time she had to check the divorced box when declaring her marital status, every time she told someone she was a divorcee, she felt like a loser or a failure. She also felt others were judging her in the same light. Believe me, I can relate. I felt the same way at the beginning of, during, and even after my divorce. And, I was amazed at the number of people who were more than willing to contribute to my negative self-image.

But is there truly a negative stigma attached to divorce, or are we being overly sensitive? Are people really judging us, or are we deflecting what we think about ourselves onto others? I believe it's a little bit of all of the above. Understand that

- there will always be people who will judge you unfairly. **What the Bible says about judging:** *Judge not, that you be not judged. For with what judgment you judge, you will be judged; and with the measure you use, it will be measured back to you. (Mat. 7:1—2)*

- there will always be people who will attempt to make you feel insecure (bad) about yourself. **What the Bible says about them:** *Hypocrite! First remove the plank from your own eye, and then you will see clearly to remove the speck from your brother's eye. (Mat. 7:5)*
- there will be times when we become "hypersensitive" because of our situation, allowing our emotions to rule over our better judgment, hence creating a window of opportunity for negative thoughts to enter into our life. **What the Bible says about controlling our thoughts:** *Finally, brethren, whatever things are true, whatever things are noble, whatever things are just, whatever things are pure, whatever things are lovely, whatever things are of good report, if there is any virtue and if there is anything praiseworthy— meditate on these things. (Phi. 4:8)*

So, rather than allow our negative thoughts dictate how we view ourselves why not take the time to define for yourself: "*Who You Are*." Simply stated......I AM.

I AM.

"As you become more clear about who you really are, you'll be better able to decide what is best for you – the first time around."– Oprah Wimfrey

Too often we feel that being a part of something or connected to someone is "who we are." Some people use their job, (what they do professionally) to define who they are; some people define themselves based upon their religious affiliation or even marital status. That is why they become devastated when things change in their lives

- If that job goes away- then who am I?
- If that person leaves me – then who am I?

You need to know who you are, and what you stand for separate from anyone or anything to avoid experiencing loss when you are separated from that life which once defined you.

We feel judged when things in our lives don't go as planned. We feel apologetic when "who" we are in the eyes of the public becomes tarnished. We allow others to make us feel uncomfortable in our own skin because we failed to live up to their expectations. The next time that you feel insecure or insignificant – Ask yourself

- why am I ashamed of who I am?
- what do I have to prove?
- who am I trying to convince that I'm worthy of respect them or me?

The bottom line is: The only person who truly needs to know who you are and what you stand for is "You."

What the Bible says about defining yourself to others:

I am the Lord, that is my Name; And my glory I will not give to another, Nor My praise to carved images. (Isa. 42:8).

Jesus' instructions to the prophets before sending them out to preach the word, *"And, whoever will not receive you nor hear your words, when you depart from that house or city, shake off the dust from your feet."(Mat. 10:13)*

Why is it important to define who you are for yourself? Because your self-esteem (self-confidence, self-worth) is linked to how you view yourself. Therefore

If	Then
You project an image of self-loathing	People will treat you lowly
You conduct yourself with dignity And self-respect	Others will treat you with dignity and respect
You allow others to determine "Who You are"	You will find yourself constantly adjusting your image, words and deeds to appease your "judges."
You don't define your life	You will miss out on life
You define yourself by your Marital status	You lose perspective about life when the marriage ends

Mama used to say: "*Act the way that you want to be treated.*" Meaning people follow your lead and will treat you according to how you present yourself.

Take Away: You have ownership of yourself. Only you can define who you are. There is no need to feel embarrassed because of your divorce. Remember

- there is no shame in taking action to ensure the best life possible for yourself or for your children, even if that action requires you to walk away from your marriage
- there is no shame in walking away from a hopeless situation when you know in your heart you've done all that you knew to do in order to make it work
- there is no shame when someone who no longer wishes to be a part of your life chooses to exit your life; and
- there is no shame in seeking counseling to help you work out those negative self-images

Emotional Benefit: Empowerment. Only, you possess the power to define your life; therefore, "*No one can make you feel inferior without your consent.*" - Eleanor Roosevelt.

Now, let's move forward in our discussion to explore the main contributor to low self-esteem or a distorted self-image—**guilt.**

GUILT

Guilt

What the Bible Says:

Then the Lord said to Cain, "Where is Abel your brother?" He said, "I do not know. Am I my brother's keeper?"

And He said, "What have you done?" The voice of your brother's blood cries out to me from the ground (Gen. 4:9-10)

Then they said to one another, "We are truly guilty concerning our brother, for we saw the anguish of his soul when he pleaded with us, and we would not hear; therefore this distress has come upon us."(Gen. 42:21)

Why are you feeling guilty? I felt guilty while working through my divorce because

- I believed that I could have done more to make the marriage better.
- I felt as if I had let my husband down by not being the best wife I could have been.

How Do You Overcome Guilt?

Start by addressing the issue. **What the Bible Says:** *For all have sinned and fall short of the Glory of God (Rom. 3:23).* Without the love of God in our life, we cannot become whole again. Know that the only way to right a wrong is to take the initiative to correct the situation. Take action to overcome your guilty feelings by incorporating the following principles I developed for myself

• **The Shoulda, Woulda, Coulda Rule** — Identify the problem, Identify possible solutions, take action to implement the solution to the problem. Ask yourself

If	Then
You don't identify the problem	How do you know what needs to be corrected
You don't identify the solution	How do you correct the problem?
You don't take the initiative, and	How can you ever resolve the issue?
Take action after you have Identified the problem, and come Up with a solution	

• **Ask for forgiveness.** If possible, go to the person you have offended and ask for forgiveness. Be prepared for rejection. Know that God will always forgive your sin and he expects you to go forward and sin no more; however, man is not always willing or - depending on the nature of your transgression and the individual's level of offense taken—even capable of forgiveness. In this situation, know that just asking for forgiveness leads you down the path of righteousness, (Walking in the Spirit). It also removes your guilt and frees you to forgive yourself.

• **Cut yourself a break!** Forgive yourself. We can't all be mental giants. Often we don't know what is the right thing to do and we aren't always aware that we are causing others pain.

Take away: If you do nothing at all the situation won't change. You have to take action in order to eliminate your guilt or obtain forgiveness.

Emotional Benefit: Freedom from Guilt. You can't change the past, but you can correct your behavior to avoid repeating the same mistakes in the future.

I recommend prayer -and possibly some professional counseling -to help you get over this next negative emotion. Bow your head, close your eyes, and repeat after me: "Our Father who is in heaven, please soften my heart and give me the strength to let go of my **resentment**."

RESENTMENT

Pity Party of One, Your Table Is Ready

What the Bible Says:

Reproach has broken my heart,
and I am full of heaviness;
I looked for someone to take pity, but there was none;
and for comforters, but I found none. (Psa. 69:20)

I gave you the best years of my life! Yeah, well who asked you to?
—Gwendolyn Carlton-Haynes

In my point of view, resentment comes when you feel slighted. We feel used, believing we sacrificed our hopes and dreams, wants and needs and didn't receive the anticipated appreciation or response from the beneficiaries of our efforts. Feeling rejected and angry, we take on a self-pitying attitude. Believe me; during those first few months working through the divorce process your need to be *understood* becomes strong. You want people to be on your side, to hear your story, so they can clearly see that you have been *victimized*. Or that you were *forced* to take some destructive *action* that caused the marriage to decompose because you were not *satisfied* or properly respected. You want to tell anyone and everyone who will listen that *"It's not my fault!"* He or she is to blame. They did not *love* me enough, or *comfort* me enough, or just simply *ignored* me.

As my marriage came to a close, not only did I sink into self-pity, I wallowed in it. I lost appreciation for the good things that were a part of our marriage, choosing instead to focus only on the negative aspects of our relationship or my spouse's character, (my favorite activity). Interestingly enough, in each scenario I was the good guy, the one who sacrificed all for the sake of the relationship. Conveniently, omitted were those times I behaved selfishly and my spouse took the high road or sacrificed his wants and needs, succumbing to my desires. **Mama used to say,** *"If you want to be happy, serve others without expectation of anything in return."* Mama was talking about unconditional love. When you do things for others without anticipation of something in return, you are practicing *unconditional l*ove. When you do something for someone with the expectation of winning favor or love, then you are practicing *conditional* love. If Mama were alive today, I'm sure she would remind us, "*that acts of support and kindness should never be measured or counted,*" and that you should readily want to please others and not consider what you do a sacrifice. There should be no strings attached to love!

So let's talk about **love.**

Don't Regret having Loved

What the Bible Says:

Love suffers long and is kind; love does not envy; love does not parade itself, is not puffed up;

does not behave rudely, does not seek its own, is not provoked, thinks no evil;

does not rejoice in iniquity, but rejoices in the truth; bears all things, believes all

things, hopes all things, endures all things. Love never fails. But whether there are

prophecies, they will fail; whether there are tongues, they will cease; whether there is knowledge, it will vanish away. (1 Cor. 13:4-8)

What is love?
According to 1 Corinthians 13:4-8 love
- should be all consuming (all or nothing)
- surpasses lust, and physical attraction
- should be given wholehearted, and vigorously regardless of the circumstances

How does God see love?
According to the Bible
- God expects us to love genuinely. **What the Bible Says:** *Let love be without hypocrisy. (Rom. 12:9).*

- God requires us to love Him. **What the Bible Says:** *And you shall love the LORD your God with all your heart, with all your soul, with all your mind, and with all your strength."This is the first commandment. (Mar. 12:30).*
- God expects us to love one another, friends and enemies alike. **What the Bible Says:** *And the second, like it, is this:"You shall love your neighbor as yourself."There is no other commandment greater than these. (Mar. 12:31).*
- God even questions, if we can truly love him, if we don't love each other. **What the Bible Says:** *If someone says, I love God, and hates his brother, he is a liar; for he who does not love his brother whom he has seen, how can he love God whom he has not seen? And, this commandment we have from Him: that he who loves God must love his brother also. (1Jn. 4:20-21).*

Question: If the Bible teaches us that love should be given freely, and unconditionally, as stated in 1 Corinthians 13:8, and according to the Bible God commands us first to love him and second to love one another then should we regret having loved – simply because the marriage has failed?

Asking someone to walk in love as described in 1 Corinthians 13:4-8 can be a hard pill to swallow when going through or after a divorce. Sure, we all felt that undying commitment at the 'beginning' of our marriage when it was young and fresh but what about now? Now, that

- angry words have been spoken

- lawyers have been hired
- the courts are in session, or
- the divorce decree has been issued?

But, there is a difference between acts of love versus being in love. The things that you did in support of your spouse during your marriage were as a result of your being in love (heartfelt, genuine expressions of love). Treating others with respect and kindness are acts of love. Don't regret having loved because the marriage has ended. Allowing God to come into your life means opening up your heart to love regardless of the circumstances. When your focus is love there is no room in your heart for regret. After all, *there is no benefit to mourning expended time.*

Take-Away: When it comes to love
- we are blessed that God loves us even if we don't deserve it and that he does not require us to be perfect in order to 'earn' his love
- you don't have to *be in love* to do loving things (*acts of love*).
- you are required to love one another regardless of the circumstances.
- don't regret having loved simply because the relationship didn't work out.

Emotional Benefit: Happiness. You have to let go of the pity party if you want to be happy. Release the negative thoughts in your head and replace them with positive self-images. Take control of your actions and thoughts.

If you truly wish to let go of resentment, start by changing how you view life. I'm talking about **letting go of unrealistic expectations**.

Letting Go of Unrealistic Expectations

What the Bible Says:

All things come alike to all:
One event happens to the righteous and the wicked;
To the good, the clean, and the unclean;
To him who sacrifices and him who does not sacrifice.
As is the good, so is the sinner;
He who takes an oath as he who fears an oath. (Ecc. 9:2)

What are we truly entitled to from life? In America the **Declaration of Independence** states that we are entitled to *the pursuit of happiness.* Note: It does not guarantee it. No one can. And the Declaration of Independence doesn't offer a game plan of how to obtain happiness, because the decision to be happy is a personal choice.

I've discovered that at those times when I experienced disappointment in the past, it was because I was harboring unrealistic expectations about the situation. So let's remove the blinders; put aside our uneducated guesses, hurt, anger, foolish pride, and resentment; then figure out what should we realistically expect out of life. Ask yourself?

- what am I entitled to before, during, and after the divorce?
- what should I expect from my ex or soon-to-be ex-spouse?
- what should I expect from my children?

What Are You Entitled to Before, During, or After Divorce?

What the Bible Says:

Furthermore it has been said, "Whoever divorces his wife, let him give her a certificate of divorce."(Mat. 5:31)

It's funny how life changes us. At the beginning of our time together, my husband and I walked down the aisle eager to pledge our love for one another. However, after the wedding vows were broken, a new set of vows—based on selfish agendas—emerged. During the divorce process, you vow *to hate, reject, and disrespect one another till the divorce decree says you are officially parted.* In other words, **let's get ready to rumble.**

What should you expect from your spouse after the divorce process? As stated above in Matthew 5:31, we should expect a certificate of divorce. However, today we envision obtaining a little more than a certificate. Although the couple will receive a divorce decree when everything is said and done, we have far more lucrative expectations: **We want half!**

I also found that sometimes the basis of resentment in my heart was due to a lack of understanding. In other words, I simply had unrealistic expectations about what a person owed me or what the outcome should have been to a particular situation. So it's not such an unusual assumption to think that you will be entitled to half of the marital assets. Of course, getting half seems doable, equitable, and fair but what does the law say?

If you are at the beginning of your divorce, this is where your attorney's expertise pays off. What you are legally entitled to depends on where you live, the divorce laws for that state, the length of the marriage, what marital assets/liabilities were accrued during that time period, how your accounts were established and property deeded, and who can legally declare (prove) ownership. So rather than speculate about what you are entitled to, take the time to do the following

- **learn about legal separations.** If you are at the beginning of the divorce process, research separation laws in your state. Learn the advantages and disadvantages of a separation agreement.

- **learn about the divorce process.** How will your spouse be served the divorce papers? How long will the process take? Is there a cooling-down period? Some states require a six-month or even one-year cooling-down period prior to ending the marriage. Will you have to go to court? How much will it cost? Learn about attorney retainer costs and fees (services breakdown – some attorney charge for their time in increments of 15, 30 or 45 minutes whether you are face-to-face or talking on the telephone). If you decide to use a paralegal, research his or her credentials as well as legal limitations.

- **learn the language of divorce**. Research the legal terminology associated with divorce so that you will be knowledgeable when interacting with your attorney and the courts.

- **learn how to make the most of your time.** Time is money, so maximize your time with your attorney, financial advisor, and accountant by
  - making copies of financial documents statements from your 401Ks and mutual funds, tax returns, payroll stubs for both you and your spouse,
  - making copies of property deeds and mortgage statements
  - bringing bank statements and make a list of account numbers for checking, savings, credit, and debit cards
  - have copies of your retirement, life insurance policies, wills, trusts documentation, and health insurance policies
  - make a list of all your liabilities and assets (autos, jewelry, rental property, timeshares, etc.)
  - document your monthly obligations (rent or mortgage payments, electricity, gas, internet services, cell phone bills, grocery, car payments, insurance for auto and home, etc.) and when possible have copies of the actual bills
  - write down important questions and concerns so they can be addressed.

- **Learn how to create a financial overview.** Take time to capture (develop a spreadsheet) your debt, banking, credit card, and insurance information so you know what you own (to ensure equitable distribution of the assets) and have a clear understanding of the financial support you'll need from your spouse to maintain your present quality of life (especially if you have children).

- **Learn about debt.** Segregate marital debt from individual debt and identify responsibilities.
- **Learn how to communicate.** Learn how to negotiate for what you want and need. Learn how to show and receive respect by effectively communicating your wants and needs.

Divorce is all about change. Suddenly, your secure world becomes unstable, therefore, when you take the time to understand how the divorce process works in your area, identify what you are entitlements under the laws in your state, and how to get the most bang for your buck when you meet with your attorney you'll feel some sense of control during an uncertain period of your life.

Take-Away: When you get involved in preserving your future, you walk away feeling victorious regardless of the outcome. So my best advice would be, *"don't get mad, get knowledge!"* And, if you manage to get everything – sweet! Just kidding!

Truthfully, the goal of this chapter is to encourage you to get knowledge about what is happening in your life, so that you won't feel disappointed or harbor hate and anger in your heart because you assumed that you would receive everything that you wanted- only to learn that legally- you have no entitlement. Take the initiative to learn about the divorce process in your state to ensure that your basic needs are met while working through the divorce, and that you will live comfortably after the dust has settled and the divorce decree issued.

Keep in mind, God can't dwell in a hate filled heart. God requires us always to walk in love. This is not about fighting to the death. And, it's not about crippling someone financially. It's about doing what is right to obtain peace of mind, and a sense of financial stability, during your struggle to rebuild your life. **What the Bible Says:** *So whoever knows the right thing to do and fails to do it, for him it is sin. (Jas. 4:17)*

Emotional Benefit: Self-respect. If you take these simple steps, you'll know what to expect and you'll gain a sense of control, self-worth, and pride because you have taken action to preserve you and your children's future.

This is a tricky one! What should you **realistically expect from your ex?**

What Can You Realistically Expect from Your Ex or Soon-To-Be Ex?

What the Bible Says:

Let your gentleness be known to all men. The Lord is at hand. (Phi. 4:5)

It seems he or she has been a part of your life forever. He or she was there when your first child was born. He or she was there to help you celebrate when you received that promotion you worked so hard to attain. He or she was there to hold your hand when your mom died and a few years later wiped the tears from your eyes as your dad was laid to rest. You've attended countless family reunions, weddings, baby showers, communions, graduations, and funerals together.

But now that things have changed, you find yourself wondering what happens next? Now that you aren't legally bound to each other, what kind of support (financial, mental, or physical) should you expect from your ex?

When my spouse first expressed that he wanted a divorce, I was so shocked I didn't know how to interact with him from that time forward. The situation was complicated even further because his announcement was so abrupt he hadn't made arrangements for separate housing.

Since we resided together at the beginning of the divorce, I found myself wishing that one day I would arrive home from my long commute from work, open the door, and find that somehow time had reversed, and we had slipped back into our old way of life, as if nothing had transpired. But, that was unrealistic.

Although, it hurt to admit it - the truth of the matter is -my spouse had established a new life for himself, and no longer felt legally, morally, or, in some instances, ethically obligated to act in my best interest; Therefore, I had to let go of my unrealistic expectations about my ex-spouse. I had to come to grips with these simple facts

- **He had moved on**. He no longer considered himself my husband and therefore did not feel obligated to look out for my best interests.
- **Life had changed.** What we once had no longer existed. I no longer had the luxury to be naïve about life, the status of my marriage, or the commitment level of my spouse.
- **No one owes you anything.** Therefore, take care of yourself.

Take-Away: It's hard to accept change, but it's not impossible. Focus your attention on what you can control, what you are legally entitled to, and let go of those things that are out of your control.

Emotional Benefit: Self-respect. Accepting the truth about your relationship with your ex or soon to be ex-spouse allows you to release unrealistic expectations about your relationship.

Leave the past in the past. Choose instead focus on loving your children, cherishing family and friends and learning how to love you.

Well, at least I can **expect the children** to be on my side, right? Um, maybe...

What Should You Expect From Your Children?

What the Bible Says:

Whoever causes one of these little ones who believe in Me to sin, it would be better for him if a millstone were hung around his neck, and he were drowned in the depth of the sea. (Mat. 18:6)

Ponder this: Every time that you take pot shots at each other — your children die inside.

- Gwendolyn Carlton-Haynes

It has always amazed me how even the youngest child can be acutely aware of his or her environment. You would be surprised what life lessons you can learn from a kindergartener. And don't get me started talking about the wisdom that spews out of the mouth of third-grader. Your children are people too they

- **Observe your behavior.** They are mini versions of you, walking, talking, acting, and thinking just like mom and dad. They are like little paparazzi, recording everything you say and do, then playing it back to any audience without your permission, and often to your embarrassment.

- **Obtain their views about life from listening to your conversations.** They inherit your prejudices about life, people, places, and things; they mimic your hate, anger, frustration, and vindictiveness.

- **Have feelings just like you.** They love, hurt, become disappointed, experience anxiety, feel embarrassed, contemplate suicide, think negative thoughts, and formulate their opinions about life and people based on cues from mom and dad.
- **Love both of their parents,** regardless of the current situation.

You should strive to conduct yourself with dignity and respect in front of your children. You should be their role model, showing them how to conduct themselves not only in good times but during adversity, and providing them an example of proper communication in a relationship. **What the Bible Says:** *And you, fathers, do not provoke your children to wrath, but bring them up in the training and admonition of the Lord. (Eph. 6:4)*

You should not expect your children to

- hate your spouse or take sides,
- become your confidante or step in and act as your parent or spouse substitute,
- take care of your emotional needs or resolve your insecurities,
- not have an opinion about what's going on in the family or be concerned about how it will impact their lives,

- not be (negatively) impacted by the breakdown of their nuclear family, or
- automatically accept new additions to the family (Dad or Mom's new partner or other children).

Although my parents never divorced, I remember how I felt as a child anytime they weren't getting along: anxious, uncertain about the stability of the family, fearful, sleepless, and helpless (when listening to Mom cry in the night believing that everyone was asleep). Depression would come over me when one parent was absent from the home or when the feeling of hostility and sorrow were pungent in the air. When my parents weren't working together in the home, the atmosphere was heavy. Folks, never underestimate your children's awareness.

Take-Away: Divorce affects everyone in the family, so think twice about the decisions you make and how they will impact those you love. As the adult, it is your job to love, protect, and set a positive example for your children, and if necessary provide them with professional counseling to help them cope during this uncertain time.

Emotional Benefit: Be a role model for your children. How you conduct yourself during times of adversity sets the standard for your children to follow. They learn coping skills by observing the actions, words, and deeds of the adults in their lives. Children who feel nurtured, loved, and secure grow up to become nurturing, loving, and self-confident adults.

Ready? Roll-up your sleeves, and grab a box of tissues because it's time to - **let go of your resentment.**

Letting Go of Resentment

What the Bible Says:

An angry man stirs up strife, and a furious man abounds in transgression. (Pro. 29:22)

Question: When you were a child, what did you dream of becoming? Are you living that dream now?

Question: When you got married, what type of marriage did you envision? How did that vision play out?

The point I'm trying to make is that life doesn't always work out the way we imagined:

- sometimes we are fortunate to realize our dreams
- sometimes our dreams never materialize
- sometimes our dreams are replaced with bigger and better dreams
- sometimes our dreams are waylaid due to the complications of life
- sometimes we choose to let go of our dreams, and "settle" taking the easier path

What happens? **Free will.** We all have choices in life. And the choices we make can determine when or if our dreams will come to fruition. The same can be said for a marriage:.

- sometimes we appreciate the struggle it took to lay the foundation for a good marriage
- sometimes we cherish the end result, we take pride and joy in the marriage we have built, and
- sometimes we are willing to do whatever it takes to maintain the relationship

However, there are times when we become bored and want to move on, perhaps taking on another partner in hopes of recapturing the drama, euphoria, and excitement we experienced in the early stages of our current (or previous) marriage.

When you are married, not only do you have to consider your dreams; you have to consider the dreams of your mate. He or she, too, has free will. He or she also had dreams as a child. He or she also had a dream of the perfect spouse, and what they imagined a fulfilling life would entail. Your ex or soon-to-be ex believed he or she made the right choice at that time. But just like everything in life, our dreams evolve. And just like you, your spouse is struggling to understand what he or she wants out of life. What seemed clear to him or her about your life together at the beginning may be now be clouded. What can you do? What should you do?

- accept the fact that your life has changed
- use this life change as an opportunity to live your dream
- take control of your life by choosing to be happy

Take-Away: You cannot make anyone love you who don't. And, you can't make anyone stay with you who wish to leave.

I hope you choose to love yourself and take this life change as an opportunity to do something fresh and exciting. Remember, with God in your life, all things are possible!

Emotional Benefit: Your decision to make the most of where you are in life opens the door to happiness. The pursuit of happiness isn't a distance race; it's a mental decision.

As in all life situations, you have to make a choice. The question is, if given a choice, **which life would you choose**?

If You Had a Choice, Which Life Would You Choose?

What the Bible Says: *Behold, I set before you today a blessing and a curse: the blessing, if you obey the commandments of the Lord your God which I command you today; and the curse, if you do not obey the commandments of the Lord your God, but turn aside from the way which I command you today, to go after other gods which you have not known. (Deu. 11:26–28)*

If you had a choice, which life would you choose? Take the quiz below. Place an X next to the statement (s) that best reflect your vision of life.

_____ Walk in peace, study, and apply the Word of God in your daily life.

_____ Hold onto hate and anger. Continue to carry the burden of resentment in your hear and spirit.

_____ Live in the past, holding onto old hurts and disappointments and finding new things to add to your disappointment list.

_____ Walking in the Spirit and loving others unconditionally

_____ Let go of the past and begin a new life grounded in peace, love, and happiness that a relationship with God can bring.

You do have a choice.

You don't have to allow resentment to take over your life and rob you of peace, love, happiness, and joy. Remember, there is no shame in feeling the way you do. We all have asked ourselves these questions

- **Do I have a right to be angry about how my life turned out?** Sure. There are times in our lives when we have given too much of ourselves and were taken for granted.

- **Do I have a right to feel resentment?** Why not? At some point, we all have some beef about how our lives turned out and would like to point the figure at our ex-spouse and say, "You did this to me."

- **Am I blameless?** No way. We have a role to play in everything that occurs in our life. Either we were an enabler, a willing participant, a passive-aggressive force, or a self-imposed victim. Whatever our role in the situation, we have to take accountability for our part.

- **Does this make me a bad person?** Not at all. It just means that you were doing the best you could do at that time. Your decisions were formulated from knowledge gained through life experiences, internal and external environmental influences, as well as your level of emotional maturity.

How do you get over resentment?

By being honest with yourself about how you feel. If you feel like crying, cry. If you feel like screaming, scream. If you feel like yelling, yell. Learn to **accept where you are in life**

right now! Learn how to feel and be honest about your feelings. It's OK to acknowledge feelings of hurt, anger, or resentment.

Too often when I talked with people about my emotions at the beginning of my divorce, they couldn't understand why I had such a hard time getting over it. But I wasn't ready or even capable at the time of letting go. I was sad, and I wanted to be sad. I was angry and wondered why I couldn't be allowed to feel anger. I was hurt and why shouldn't I be hurt? Hadn't I been treated poorly? Wasn't life ugly for me now? After all, I am a human being. My advice: Go for it. Get it all out! I bet that felt good, didn't it? Honesty is the best policy.

Take-Away: Now that you've gotten all of that pent-up negative energy out of take the following empowering actions

- **Stop holding onto self-pity.** You don't need it. You are intelligent, strong, and self-reliant.
- **Stop expecting unrealistic entitlements.** You don't need to manipulate, coerce, or control anyone into being with you. Honestly, nobody owes you anything.
- **Stop giving love conditionally.** This is not keeping in alignment with the Word of God.
- **Stop creating unnecessary strife** in your life, your children's lives, and your ex's life because you refuse to let go of hate, anger, and the need for revenge.
- **Start letting go of those negative emotions.** You don't need them anymore. You've identified what

you're feeling. You've indulged those emotions. Now release them. They have no place in your future.

Emotional Benefit: When you stop hating, you open up your heart to give and receive love.

Everyone knows you can't truly release resentment until you **let go of hate and anger.**

HATE & ANGER

Let the Hating Begin

What the Bible Says:

And whenever you stand praying, if you have anything against anyone, forgive him, that your Father in heaven may also forgive you your trespasses. But if you do not forgive, neither will your Father in heaven forgive your trespasses. (Mar.11:25—26)

I hate you.

I am angry with you because you did not appreciate or respect our marriage. I am angry with you because you are saying and doing things that I don't understand and can't respect, and as a result, I am forced to defend myself to others. I am angry with you because I sacrificed my life by marrying you in the first place, ignoring the voice of reason in my head. As a matter of fact, I am angry with you because I didn't leave you years ago.

I hate you because I still need your love, crave your touch, and want your affection, even though you have moved on to pursue other people. I hate you because you cheated on me and I can no longer trust you. I hate you because when I had the opportunity to cheat on you, I respected the sanctity of our marriage and remained faithful. I hate you because your actions have caused me to start my life over; I had planned to spend the rest of my life with you. I hate you because you will no longer be a part of my life. I hate you. I hate you. I hate you.

What does the Bible say about hating others?

He who says he is in the light, and hates his brother, is in darkness until now. He who loves his brother abides in the light, and there is no cause for stumbling in him. But he who hates his brother is in darkness and walks in darkness, and does not know where he is going, because the darkness has blinded his eyes. (1 Jn. 2:9—11)

I hate me.

I hate me because I feel helpless without you. I hate me because I became so overcome with grief when you left that I could not get out of bed in the morning. I hate me because I took great pains to look, and behave differently from my true self, in order to keep you in my life. I hate me because I denied myself the true relationship that I craved, in order to remain by your side. I hate me because I still think about you and want you in my life. I hate me because foolish pride is keeping me from crying even though I want and need to cry. I hate me because I still want you even though I know you are not good for me, and we cannot have a healthy relationship on any level. I hate me. I hate me. I hate me.

What does the Bible say about self-loathing?

Put away from you a deceitful mouth.
And put perverse lips far from you. (Pro. 4:24)

Breathe!

You have to let the hate out. It is only human to hate. I experienced hate and anger when

- **I felt powerless about a situation.** Try as I might, I could not control the destruction of our marriage. I could not stop the departure of my mate. I could not halt the rush of emotions that flooded my heart at the thought of him leaving and having to start over.

- **I felt slighted**. I had sacrificed myself for another without obtaining the anticipated response.

- **I felt restrained**. I had trouble coping with the disappointment and didn't know how to move past the pain.

Allow yourself to let the hate out, then make a decision to act in peace and conduct yourself with dignity, and respect before, during, and after the divorce. Don't become that bitter man or woman who talks about his or her divorce so vividly, and with such pain, and suffering that one would think it happened only two days ago when in reality it occurred over ten years ago! What a waste of time!

Take-Away: Strive to do what is right, thereby eliminating the need to seek revenge.

Keep in mind that your self-worth is not linked to the marriage's success or failure or whether your spouse is absent or present in your life.

Emotional Benefit: Changing how you view the world will lighten your heart, and save your life. There should be no strings attacht your marriage. Take pride in the fact that in your role as a husband or wife you did what was required of you biblically by

- loving, honoring, and respecting your spouse, and
- upholding the sanctity of the marriage.

Know that your life isn't over just because you are divorced.

Psst, want to know a secret? I can tell you the **truth about hate and anger.**

The Truth About Hate and Anger

What the Bible Says:

The Lord is merciful and gracious,
slow to anger, and abounding in mercy (Psa. 103.8)

Let all bitterness, wrath, anger, clamor, and evil speaking be put away from you, with all malice. And be kind to one another, tender-hearted, forgiving one another, even as God in Christ forgave you. (Eph. 4:31–32)

What is the truth about harboring hate and anger in your heart?

In my opinion, *you are actually mad at yourself.* Have you ever been in an argument with someone and during the heat of the battle you became so angry at the person or situation that you could not think clearly or even utter one word? Maybe you just stood there filled with embarrassment, hate, and anger, frustrated and voiceless while he or she spewed hateful and disrespectful words toward you. Maybe that person walked away victorious, head held high, back straight, chest out, with a swagger in his or her step, visibly proud of the tongue-lashing he or she had released upon you while you just stood there red-faced, head down, shoulders drooped, helpless and defeated. And ironically, maybe the minute the argument was over and you sat alone, reliving the incident, everything you wished you could have said or done began to flow through your mind.

The cause of our anger is not always a confrontation such as the one identified above. You could feel hate and anger over your inability to respond differently in any stressful situation. Perhaps you wish you could recapture that moment so that instead of standing there like a *deer caught in the headlights,* you could say something clever, venomous, and full of sarcasm or react apathetically. What you are seeking, in essence, is to return to the situation that made you feel like a loser and change the outcome so that

- you were the one in complete control,
- you had the power to make the offending party regret his or her behavior,
- you were the victor of the battle.

Instead of limping away in shock and disappointment, you would have *flipped the script*, taken control of the situation, and changed the outcome. What you are truly angry about is your **missed opportunity** to inflict pain.

Missed Opportunities

What the Bible Says:

But sin, taking opportunity by the commandment, produced in me all manner of evil desire. For apart from the law sin was dead. (Rom. 7:8)

Why did I say that the truth about 'Hate and Anger' is that you are angry with yourself? Because for me those words were true; unfortunately, when working through a divorce you have plenty of opportunities to second-guess your decisions and more often than not you feel inadequate because you believe you should have taken a stronger approach or acted more aggressively. You regret those missed opportunities to get out all the things you wanted to say to your spouse, having chosen instead to hold your tongue. Long after the situation has passed, all you can do is sit filled with hate and anger, beating yourself up about not being able to handle yourself in an *unanticipated, unprovoked, emotionally charged* situation.

What the Bible says about...

Pride. *A man's pride will bring him low, but the humble in spirit will retain honor. (Pro. 29:23)*

Confrontations. *It is honorable for a man to stop striving, since any fool can start a quarrel. (Pro. 20:3)*

Vengeance. *Vengeance is Mine, and recompense; their foot shall slip in due time; for the day of their calamity is at hand, and the things to come hasten upon them. (Deu. 32:35)*

Taking offense. *A brother offended is harder to win than a strong city, and contentions are like the bars of a castle. (Pro. 18:19)*

Listening to your ego. *He who trusts in his own heart is a fool, but whoever walks wisely will be delivered. (Pro. 28:26)*

Evil thoughts. *The fear of the Lord is to hate evil; pride and arrogance and the evil way and the perverse mouth I hate. (Pro. 8:13)*

So what can you do? Start by **giving up on seeking revenge.**

Give Up on Seeking Revenge

What the Bible Says:

Beloved, do not avenge yourselves, but rather give place unto wrath; for it is written, "Vengeance is Mine, I will repay," says the Lord.

Therefore "if your enemy is hungry, feed him;
if he is thirsty, give him a drink;
for in so doing you will heap coals of fire on his head."
Do not be overcome by evil, but overcome evil with good. (Rom. 12:19–21)

Give up hate and anger.

Give up being angry with yourself. Give up second-guessing yourself. Let go of foolish pride. Let go of the need for revenge. You will never be able to recapture that offensive moment in time. Stop trying. Instead, redirect your efforts into diligently working toward positive goals, and attaining your aspirations. If you want to get even, do it by *"getting a life."* Turn away from hate and discontent. Don't seek to be in the presence of people who caused you pain. Let them have their small victory.

What the Bible Says:

For the turning away of the simple will slay them,
and the complacency of fools will destroy them;

but whoever listens to me will dwell safely,
and will be secure, without fear of evil. (Pro. 1:32–33).

No one wins in a fight. Sure, you may get the chance to finally confront that person who hurt you in the past. Sure, you may finally get the opportunity to say and do all those things you've wanted to for so long. However, any victory in treating someone with disrespect, inflicting hurt, and pain, will be short-lived. After the dust settles, and you're alone with your thoughts, you'll have to deal with the ugliness of your behavior. You will feel dirty because doing evil is filthy work. Guilt and shame will come upon you.

What the Bible Says:

Even a fool is counted wise when he holds his peace;
when he shuts his lips,
he is considered perceptive. (Pro. 17:28)

If you pursue revenge, you'll soon realize that people who witness your behavior will view you in a different light—as vindictive and evil, maybe even vicious! In fact, they may turn away from you because of your inability to control your behavior. Surprised, and disappointed by your lack of restraint, choice of words, actions, and deeds. Others, who don't know the cause of your animosity, toward that person may feel sorry for him or her. And, depending on your level of attack, you may have now made people feel sorry for him or her for being, *victimized* by *you*! Before you decide to move forward with your plan of revenge stop, and pray. Ask God to

- forgive you for your evil behavior and wicked thoughts,
- remove hate, and anger from your heart
- help you forgive your transgressor for his or her behavior toward you, and
- show you how to love and direct you in the right path toward forgiveness.

Then listen for God's response, and be obedient to his guidance.

Take-Away: Holding on to hate and anger is about pride. You become frustrated with yourself for

- not anticipating the actions of another,
- allowing yourself to become so paralyzed with anger you could not verbally express (defend) yourself in a hostile situation,
- allowing someone to get away with treating you disrespectfully,
- not taking advantage of the opportunity to finally confront a person or situation that has been the source of your hate and anger,
- allowing them to win, *again*.

Emotional Benefit: Emotional maturity. Once you learn that you have nothing to prove, you will discover that it is not always necessary to react negatively when confronted by others. The better person is the one who walks away from conflict. Always strive to let your actions, represent the presence of God in your life.

Question: How do you **control anger?**

Controlling Anger

What the Bible Says:

So then, my beloved brethren, let every man be swift to hear, slow to speak,

slow to wrath; for the wrath of man does not produce the righteousness of God.

Therefore lay aside all filthiness and overflow of wickedness and receive with

meekness the implanted word, which is able to save your souls. (Jas. 1:19–21)

I forgive you.

I forgive you for not being perfect. I forgive you for letting me down. I forgive you for walking out on our marriage. I applaud your courage to be true to yourself and leave despite the overwhelming pressure to remain in a marriage you no longer find satisfying. I know now that it is important for you to be true to yourself. I know now that it is important for me to forgive because there is power in forgiveness. I know now that I have to forgive you to free my soul and move forward into the future minus the baggage of the past.

I forgive me.

I forgive me for not being perfect. I forgive myself for harboring hate in my heart. I recognize that healing takes time.

I will allow myself to forgive me. I now know that it is OK to forgive. I also know that it is OK to not feel guilty about excluding people from my life whose presence causes me pain. I now understand that forgiving others releases me from the bondage of the past and eliminates feelings of pain, hurt, and anger. I have learned to turn to prayer for strength, inspiration, and guidance when I encounter pain bigger than I can handle.

In **Matthew 6:9–13**, Jesus taught his disciples how to pray as follows: "*Our Father in heaven, Hallowed be Your name. Your kingdom come. Your will be done, on earth as it is in heaven. And forgive us our debts, as we forgive our debtors, and do not lead us into temptation, but deliver us from the evil one. For Yours is the kingdom and the power and the glory forever. Amen.*"

Jesus then went on to say in **Matthew 6: 14–15**, "*For if you forgive men their trespasses, your heavenly Father will also forgive you. But if you do not forgive men their trespasses, neither will your Father forgive your trespasses.*"

Take-Away: What do these passages have to do with controlling anger? They teach you to
- let go and let God's will be done in your life,
- forgive your brother for his trespasses so that God the Father will in turn forgive you,
- not allow anger to prompt you to sin, and
- stop and pray when you feel weakness rising up in your heart.

Emotional Benefit: Walking in the Spirit (love) brings faith, hope, and peace into your life.

. It lightens your soul and opens your heart to healing.

Now that we've learned how to control our anger, let's focus on another breeding ground for hate and anger: **martyrdom**

When the Saints Go Marching In: Are You a Martyr?

What the Bible Says:

Then Paul answered, "What do you mean by weeping and breaking my heart?

For I am ready not only to be bound, but also to die at Jerusalem for the name

of the Lord Jesus." (Act. 21:13)

"I tried and I tried." When I first heard these words, I laughed so hard I thought I would fall out of my chair. During a discussion over dinner about divorce, a dear friend shared this favorite quotation from her ex-husband. Every time he wanted to impress upon others the sacrifices he had made to be a good husband even in the midst of adversity and how he had struggled to make things right in the marriage, he would start each sentence by uttering, *"I tried and I tried."* You see, he wanted to make sure that everyone knew of his selfless sacrifices, he wanted to show others that he had been victimized.

His words are the perfect example of martyrdom. What a saint, right? Well, don't judge him too harshly. After all, it is hard work being a martyr

- it requires feeling sorry for yourself.
- it involves self-sacrifice for the admiration of others.

- it involves creating and maintaining a Who Benefited from My Sacrifices? checklist.
- it involves emotional manipulation of others, aka guilt.

What's wrong with being a martyr?

Sooner or later you start resenting your role. Eventually you come to the conclusion that there is nothing to be gained by being a martyr. You want out, but you don't know how to get out of your self-imposed prison. You become angry with the people around you for taking advantage of you (according to the negative thoughts that keep popping up in your head) or for taking you for granted, allowing hate and anger to creep into your heart.

How do you let go of martyrdom? Learn how to

- **Love.** Love yourself. Love the people in your life. Do the things that make you happy, not out of guilt or obligation.
- **Let people in.** Allow others to show how much they care for you. Allow others to shower you with love and affection.
- **Stop feeling responsible for everything.** Learn how to say yes when others offer their services, money, time, and effort. Allow others to take on some of the responsibility. Allow others to contribute to the maintenance of the household. Allow others to stand up and be accountable. Learn how to accept help from others. Learn how to graciously say thank you.

- **Say no without feeling guilty**. If you feel manipulated or controlled, then stand up to the person causing you to feel that way and tell them you are not happy with how you are being treated. . If you agree to do something but have second thoughts, go to that person and say you've a change of heart. It is OK to change your mind.

- **Practice unconditional love.** Do things for others without any strings attached. Stop using self-sacrifice as a manipulation tool.

- **Keep a secret.** Break the Martyr syndrome. Do things for others without telling the world of your good deeds. If it's from the heart — it doesn't have to be announced to the world.

Working through a divorce is not the time to be a martyr. Don't sacrifice your needs in order to appease others. Work with your attorney to identify what you are legally entitled so that after the dust has settled, and the divorce is final -you will be happy with the results.

If you are divorced, the only way that you will be happy is to stop being the victim. Be satisfied with the decisions that you have made, accept where you are in life, and make a conscious decision to move on to bigger and better things. The only way to get over the past is to stop talking about it and start focusing on the future.

Take-Away: Obtain your accolades from God. Do your good works unto the Lord, meaning your good deeds should be a result of your faith and wanting to always do the right thing. Not for praise, not for pats on the back, not to show that you are a good and righteous person.

Emotional Benefit: Stop being a 'people pleaser.' There is joy in knowing that you have a right to do what is right for you (free will) and that you are entitled to say 'no' and not feel guilty or as if you are letting the world down.

Now that you've stopped being a martyr, you are ready to start letting go. How do you let go? Well, **you gotta**

CHAPTER 5:
YOU GOTTAS

Chapter 5:You Gotta: Let God be Your Guide

What the Bible Says:

For even if there are so-called gods, whether in heaven or on earth (as there are many gods and many lords), Yet for us there is one God, the Father, of whom are all things, and we for Him; and one Lord Jesus Christ, through whom are all things, and through whom we live. (1 Cor. 8:5-6)

Now that we have reached the end of our journey, I hope that you've realized that with *God as Your Guide* all things are possible, and that *Overcoming the Emotional Trauma of Divorce* can be accomplished in 5 easy Steps

- **Step One** - establish a relationship with God **(Seek God's Face).** Building a relationship with God sets the foundation for stability in your life regardless of what adversities that you may face. Remember, only God can change your heart.

- **Step Two** - allow others to be themselves **(Free will),** and learn how to take accountability for your decisions when you **Evoke** your **Free Will.**

- **Step Three** - get help **(Obtain Counsel).** Sometimes what we are experiencing emotionally is beyond the expertise of our support system (family, friends, coworkers, clergy) and it is at those times that a professional counselor can be beneficial.

- **Step Four** - acknowledge that **Negative Emotions** (disappointment, shame, guilt, resentment, hate & anger) do exist and that, it's ok to allow yourself to experience them but it's not ok to allow those negative emotions to take control of your life.

- **Step Five** - realize that you have the power to make a difference in your own life. Simply stated, steps one through four means nothing if you don't take action. In other words, **"You Gotta**........"
  - Get Over Yourself
  - Trust
  - Forgive and Forget
  - Let go

Question: How do you **get over yourself**?

You Gotta: Get Over Yourself

What the Bible Says:

Be of the same mind toward one another. Do not set your mind on high things, but associate with the humble. Do not be wise in your own opinion. (Rom. 12:16)

If you wish to overcome the emotional trauma of divorce, you need to accept these things
- you are not perfect.
- life sometimes catches you off guard, and there will be times when you won't be able to solve life's problems alone.
- people will come and go
- as long as you remain above ground, you will experience

    rejection, disappointment, hurt, pain, fear, jealousy, envy, guilt, insecurity, love, hope, joy, empowerment, peace, happiness, prosperity, passion, health, wealth, confidence, adversity, poverty, sorrow, despair, and confusion.
- life isn't always easy or, for that matter, fun.
- regardless of how you feel, God will bless your enemies just as he continues to bless you.
- God will not smite your ex just because he or she has offended you.
- you have to learn to laugh if you want to survive.

- to allow room for growth, you must let go of the need to feel sorry for yourself.
- your ex-spouse will move on with his or her life and establish new relationships, friendships, and families, and he or she will be happy without your permission.

And, you gotta learn how to trust.

You Gotta: Trust

What the Bible Says:

But the Lord said to Samuel, "Do not look at his appearance or at his physical stature, because I have refused him. For the Lord does not see as man sees; for man looks at the outward appearance, but the Lord looks at the heart. (1 Sam. 16:7)

If only we could look at people through God's eyes and know what truly resides in their hearts. What a great gift! However, there is always a flip side. That would mean *our* heart would also be fully exposed for public scrutiny. What a dilemma that would create! The truth is, when it comes to trusting one another, you gotta have faith. My motto regarding trust may be cynical at best: *I'll trust you until the"you"shows me that I should no longer extend that trust.*

What the Bible Says:

Blessed is the man who trusts in the Lord, and whose hope is the Lord. (Jer. 17:7)

It's hard to regain trust after someone you loved, honored, respected, and thought you knew let you down. This is true whether the individual is your husband, wife, family member, friend, or coworker. What can you do to regain trust for other

Homo sapiens? I have always heard that it takes time to heal. Besides, you cannot possibly know what is in another's heart.

What the Bible Says:

The heart is deceitful above all things, and desperately wicked; who can know it? (Jer.17:9)

Take-Away: The one thing we all have in common is that we are all imperfect. Today someone you respected may have let you down in an unpredictable, unexpected, and totally inappropriate manner. Tomorrow you may do the same thing to someone else. So you have a choice: You can either buy into the negative mind-set that everyone can't be trusted or make the decision

- that trusting others should be automatic until the Holy Spirit reveals to you that you should no longer extend that trust
- to appreciate what people in your life bring to the relationship rather than constantly trying to assess who they are according to your standards.

Emotional Benefit: Faith. Trust that God is the final judge and he knows when it's time for someone to leave your life. Trust God's judgment.

I know I have to **forgive** but how do I **forget**?

You Gotta: Forgive and Forget

What the Bible Says:

And be kind to one another, tenderhearted, forgiving one another, even as God in Christ forgave you. (Eph. 4:32)

Forgiving does not mean that you have to allow the trespasser to remain in your life. It means that you forgive the trespass, (action) then shake the aggression, (pain and strife) from your life to move forward.

Forgiving is for you.

It allows you to clear the air, remove any hate and anger, and move forward with your life. Forgiving is empowering. There is power in deciding to do the right thing and not allowing yourself to be hindered by the past. Forgiveness frees you from sin and allows you to connect to God. When you forgive, you no longer need to assign blame. You no longer need to hear "It's not your fault!" because it doesn't matter what happened in the past.

You Gotta Forget.

How? Start by changing the subject.

- **Stop** talking about your divorce.
- **Stop** putting down your ex to anyone who will listen.

- **Stop** playing a soundtrack in your mind of your life-disappointments greatest hits.
- **Start** letting go of foolish pride, unrealistic expectations, hurt, and pain.
- **Forget** about the life you once shared with your ex and *focus* on enjoying your *life right now!*

Take-Away: Starting over can be a blessing if you embrace where you are in life, decide to make the change work for you, and don't allow your mind to work against you. Remember

- working through a divorce is painful, frightening, and challenging, but it's not the end of the world!
- being single again is lonely and uncomfortable but it's not the end of the world!
- being disappointed that your marriage failed is common. Grieve the loss of your marriage but don't use your grief as an excuse not to grow. Quit hiding behind the pain of the past. Besides, experiencing disappointment isn't the end of the world!

Emotional Benefit: Replace pain with Love. Hopefully, by now you have learned how to love, and appreciate who you are. You've heard it said a thousand times, *"No one will love you if you don't love yourself."* Why not take the advice, and start loving *"You?"* Besides, you are kinda cute!

Drum roll, please. .... We have reached the finish line the final step in *Overcoming the Emotional Trauma of Divorce with God as Your Guide* is...... **you gotta let go.**

You Gotta: Let Go

What the Bible Says:

Not that I have already attained, or am already perfected; but I press on, that I may lay hold of that for which Christ Jesus has also laid hold of me. Brethren, I do not count myself to have apprehended; but one thing I do, forgetting those things which are behind and reaching forward to those things which are ahead, I press toward the goal for the prize of the upward call of God in Christ Jesus. Therefore let us, as many as are mature, have this mind; and if in anything you think otherwise, God will reveal even this to you. (Phi. 3:12–15)

You have gone through a tough time, but don't allow the challenges of life to
- darken your spirit and rob you of joy
- define who you are or what you will become, or distort how you view yourself

Let go of negativity.

Let those negative emotions find another home. Let go of negative people. Fill your life with positive, challenging, and innovative people and activities. Do not allow yourself to be drawn into the past. Simply change the subject or if necessary, change the company you keep. Practice open, and honest communication. Do not hide your feelings, and learn to confront a problem head on. Remember, life is indeed too short, so do not waste time being unhappy. The choice is yours to make you can

Live in Negativity	**Or**
Wishing to be healed	Take the initiative to establish a relationship with God which is your healing source
Frustrated because you can't control the actions of others	Embracing the fact that people have a right to do what is right for them (Free Will)
Trapped in the past	Connect with a therapist or counselor to learn coping techniques so that you can move on with your life free of remorse
Feeling ashamed because you are divorced	Feel proud of yourself for working through your fears
Full of resentment	Thank God for giving you the strength to face your adversities and use the experience as an opportunity to grow mentally and spiritually
Filled with hate and anger	Make a decision to be happy

Take-Away: Stop doubting yourself, and your abilities because of what you experienced during your divorce. You have what it takes, (chutzpah) to stand on your own, and start your life anew.

Remember, nothing will happen to you today that you and God can't face together.

Emotional Benefit: Let your testimony be that although the first part of your life didn't work out as you had intended but through the grace of God, the second part of your life is going full steam ahead, and it's **fa-bu-lous!**

Made in the USA
Charleston, SC
13 January 2014